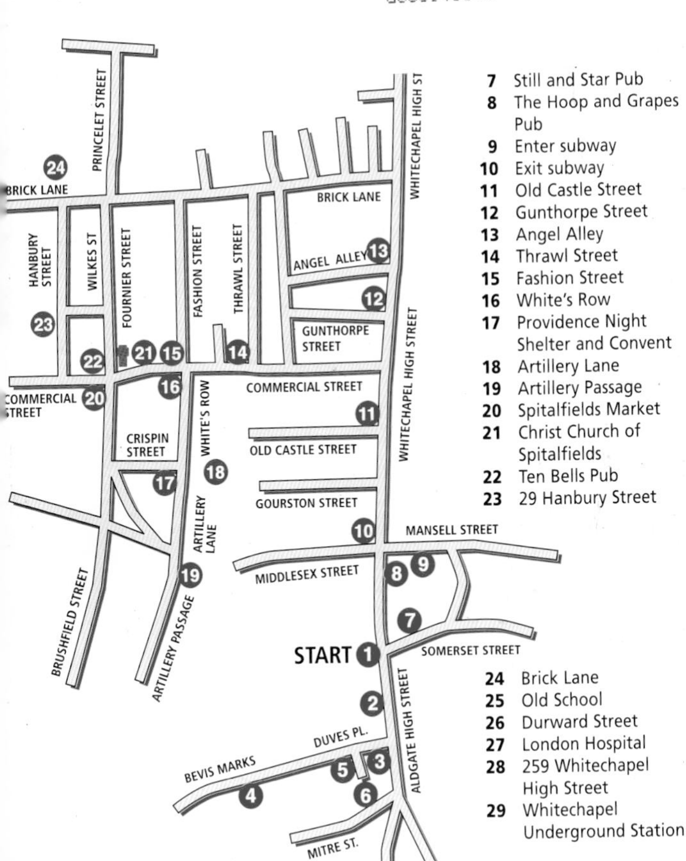
PRINCELET STREET
BRICK LANE
HANBURY STREET
WILKES ST
FOURNIER STREET
FASHION STREET
THRAWL STREET
BRICK LANE
ANGEL ALLEY
GUNTHORPE STREET
WHITECHAPEL HIGH ST
WHITECHAPEL HIGH STREET
COMMERCIAL STREET
COMMERCIAL STREET
CRISPIN STREET
WHITE'S ROW
OLD CASTLE STREET
GOURSTON STREET
ARTILLERY LANE
MANSELL STREET
MIDDLESEX STREET
BRUSHFIELD STREET
ARTILLERY PASSAGE
START
SOMERSET STREET
ALDGATE HIGH STREET
DUVES PL.
BEVIS MARKS
MITRE ST.
7 Still and Star Pub
8 The Hoop and Grapes Pub
9 Enter subway
10 Exit subway
11 Old Castle Street
12 Gunthorpe Street
13 Angel Alley
14 Thrawl Street
15 Fashion Street
16 White's Row
17 Providence Night Shelter and Convent
18 Artillery Lane
19 Artillery Passage
20 Spitalfields Market
21 Christ Church of Spitalfields
22 Ten Bells Pub
23 29 Hanbury Street
24 Brick Lane
25 Old School
26 Durward Street
27 London Hospital
28 259 Whitechapel High Street
29 Whitechapel Underground Station

OPENING TIMES

Bevis Marks Synagogue:	*Sun.- Wed.: 11.30 am to 12.30 pm*
Petticoat Lane Market:	*Early Sunday mornings only*
Brick Lane Market:	*Early Sunday mornings only*
Ten Bells Pub:	*Mon.- Sat: 12.00 noon to 11.00 pm* *Sun: 12.00 noon to 10.30 pm*
Hoop and Grapes Pub:	*Mon.- Fri: 11.00 am to 11.00 pm;* *Sat.- Sun: Closed all day*

Advice

We do not advise you to take this walk after dark.

The Walk can be done on any day of the week, but it is worth bearing in mi that the Hoop and Grapes Pub is closed at weekends and that both the marke on this Walk are held on Sunday mornings only.

START OF WALK

Directions: Start this Walk at Aldgate Underground Station (N.B. Not Aldga East), which is at the very end (East direction) of the Metropolitan Line.

Exit Aldgate Underground Station ❶. Turn right and walk down Aldgate Hig Street. Immediately on the right is the Church of St Boltoph ❷.

Church of St Boltoph: This Church dates from 1744, although there has bee a church on this site for over 1000 years. The attractive ceiling inside w designed by J.F. Bentley, who also designed the Roman Catholic Westminst Cathedral (not the Abbey). The Church's Renatus Harris organ is the oldest London and dates from 1676.

During the 1700s, the mummified body of a young boy, in a standir position, was discovered in the Church's vaults. The Church decided to rai some money and charged the public a two pence entry fee to see the spectac

Directions: Continue past the Church. Cross over the two smaller roads at th traffic lights. Turn immediately right down Dukes Place. On the left is Sir Joh Cass's Foundation School ❸.

Sir John Cass's Foundation School: Founded as a school in 1669 to educa both boys and girls. In 1710, Sir John Cass agreed to make regular financi donations to keep the School going. However, in 1718, while drawing up h second will (leaving all his money to the School), he suffered a fat haemorrhage and died. He was found with a blood-stained quill at his desk.

ıe tragedy is still commemorated each year on Founder's Day, when all the ıpils are given pens, stained red, which they wear in their lapels.

irections: Continue to walk down Dukes Place. The road becomes Bevis Marks; ontinue and, on the left, hidden within a modern building at no. 14 Bevis larks, you will see the entrance to Bevis Marks Synagogue ❹.

evis Marks Synagogue: This Synagogue was founded in 1657 and is the ıdest synagogue in London. The Synagogue has changed very little, and is a minder that the Jewish community was very large in the East End during the 7th and 18th centuries. The Synagogue has been in continual use ever since it rst opened 300 years ago.

*irections: Exit the Synagogue onto Bevis Marks and turn right, back down evis Marks the way you came, keeping on the right hand side. Stop on the orner of the third turning on the right, which is St James's Passag*❺.

t James's Passage: On this very corner, on the 30th September 1888, the ourth victim of the Ripper – Catherine Eddows – was last seen alive. She was en standing here talking to a stranger who, it is believed, must have been Jack ıe Ripper.

Catherine was a 46-year old street prostitute. She was born in Volverhampton in 1848, and when she was eight years old, her entire family alked the long journey to London to find work. Her friends and relations escribed her as "intelligent" and a "jolly woman with a fiery temper". On the ight of her murder, at around 8.00 pm, Catherine was arrested for being gloriously drunk" in Aldgate High Street and for running up and down the oad imitating a fire engine! Later that night, after being released from the olice cell, she headed back to Aldgate High Street in the hope, it is believed, f finding a client to raise some money for a bed for that night.

Early that morning at 1.30 am, Joseph Lawende and a friend were leaving a ewish working men's club in Duke Street, which was at the opposite side of litre Square ❻. As they walked through St James's Passage, they saw a man nd a woman, standing on the corner. Catherine was touching the man's chest. s the two men passed the couple, it was obvious to them that Catherine was ecoming increasingly more friendly with the man. Catherine's mutilated body as found twenty minutes later, only yards away, in Mitre Square.

It was clear from the vivid eye witness accounts, clothing of the victim found t the murder scene and the evidence at the post-mortem, that Catherine ddows was the woman seen on the corner and was the victim. It was also clear ıat the man she had been seen with – described by the witnesses as having a ark moustache and wearing a tweed-jacket, deer stalker cap and red neckscarf was Jack the Ripper himself. These witnesses are thought to be the only two eople to have seen the Ripper at work and lived to tell the tale.

Directions: Continue into St James's Passage which leads into Mitre Square ❻ Walk directly ahead to the far left corner of the Square and stop at the iro gates on the left. Notice the original cobblestones.

Mitre Square: *Murder Site of Catherine Eddows*

Less than twenty minutes after Catherine was last seen, PC Watkins walke into the Square from Mitre Street, which is just ahead. He shone h lantern into this dark corner of the Square and could just make out a pool c blood and a woman's body sprawled out on the cobblestones next to a woode gate. Even in the darkness he could see that she had been cut to pieces an terribly mutilated. He blew his whistle and, within minutes,a crowd of peop had arrived to witness the body of the Ripper's fourth victim.

How could a woman be murdered without anyone hearing her screams? A the post-mortem, it was found that Catherine had an eight-inch slash across he throat, which had cut her vocal chords. The other more gruesome and terrifyin mutilations had been done after her death.

Mitre Square was originally founded in 1108 by Matilda of Scotland, the wif of Henry I. The Square marked the site of the cloisters of the Priory of the Ho Trinity. A ghostly figure of a woman has often been seen by people taking short cut home late at night. The ghost is seen lying on the cobblestones nex to the gate, the exact spot where Catherine's body was found.

Directions: Exit Mitre Square into Mitre Street. Turn left and walk to the end c Mitre Street. Turn left along Fenchurch Street heading back to the Church of S Boltoph ❷. Continue a little further back to Aldgate Underground Station ❶ Cross the road at the traffic lights, which are outside the Underground Statior Turn left after you have crossed the road and immediately on the right ente Somerset Street, which is in fact a small enclosed alley. A little further on the le you will come to the Still and Star Pub ❼.

Still and Star Pub: There are probably only two pubs in England with thi unusual name. This Pub and its immediate surroundings were thought to hav been linked to Jack the Ripper because, surrounding this Pub during the 1880s were dozens of slaughter houses. One theory was that Jack the Ripper was butcher and that he would have worked in this area and probably drank here The Pub remains the same as it did during the Ripper's days, but the rest of th area has changed a great deal, so that even Jack the Ripper would not recognis it today.

Directions: return the way you have just come, through Somerset Street t Aldgate High Street. Turn right. A little further along on the right, on the corne of Mansell Street is the Hoop and Grapes Pub ❽.

Hoop and Grapes Pub: This is the oldest surviving pub in London and would have been in business in the time of the Ripper. The building was originally a private house, built in the early 1600s and is well worth a look inside. The Hoop and Grapes Pub was one of the few buildings to have survived the Great Fire of London in 1666, in which over 80% of houses were burnt to the ground. Look at the wooden carvings at the entrance as you enter and the wooden overhanging upper gallery. Notice how narrow the Pub is inside.

Like many of the inns from this period there are large cellars and underground passages. The secret passages underneath this Pub are said to be linked to the Tower of London and the River Thames; many river pirates and smugglers were known to have worked on this part of the river.

Directions: *Continue along Aldgate High Street. Turn immediately right, into Mansell Street. Immediately in front of you is the Subway* **9**.

Enter the subway. Continue along and make sure you turn into the first intersection on the left. Continue, and turn first left up the stairs to exit the subway **10** *on Whitechapel High Street.*

Behind the Subway is Middlesex Street, better known as Petticoat Lane. There has been a market here since 1608 (Sundays mornings only). As you exit the Subway, continue straight ahead down Whitechapel High Street, keeping to the left. Stop on the corner of the first street on the left, which is Goulston Street.

Goulston Street: Following the murder of Catherine Eddows, it was noticed at her post-mortem, that a piece of her blood-stained dress was missing. The missing material was discovered a few hours after her murder in a passageway at no. 108-119 Goulston Street. The passageway today has been blocked off. On the back wall of the passage there was a message written in chalk saying: "The Juwes are not the men that will be blamed for nothing". The Police Commissioner rubbed out the message shortly after arriving on the scene. Later, he explained his actions by saying that he thought the message would inflame anti-Jewish feeling in the area.

On the corner of Goulston Street, you may see Tubby Isaacs' world famous eel stall. Well worth a try if you want to taste some traditional East End food. Tubby opens and closes his stall at irregular times.

Directions: *Continue along Whitechapel High Street. Next on the left is Old Castle Street* **11**.

Old Castle Street: ***Murder Site of Alice McKenzie***

Alice was also known by the name "clay pipe Alice". Her murder took place on 17th July 1889 (at least six months after the murder which has been officially acknowledged as the Ripper's last). However, similarities exist between the McKenzie murder and the other murders and so many believe she was probably actually Jack the Ripper's last victim.

On the night of her murder, Alice went out to work with another prostitute called "Mog Cheeks". Both women needed to earn some money, to be able to afford a bed for the night. Nothing is known about what happened before the murder other than the two friends were separated early in the evening.

PC Andrews turned into Old Castle Street and just inside the entrance, under a market barrow, he found the mutilated body of Alice McKenzie. Her throat had been cut from ear-to-ear in typical Ripper style and her abdomen had been opened up, so that what was inside was now on the outside. Alice still had her possessions in her pocket, a clay pipe and one silver farthing – probably everything she owned in the world.

Directions: *Continue along Whitechapel High Street and cross over Commercial Street at the traffic lights and continue. Stop at the second alley on the left, which is called Gunthorpe Street* **12**.

Gunthorpe Street: *Murder Site of Martha Turner*

This was another murder about which people were, and still are, unsure. Turner's murder happened on 6th August 1888, several months before the first official Ripper murder. However, the person who killed Martha used the same equipment as the Ripper and there were similar mutilations as the murders that followed; so there is every possibility that she too was killed by Jack the Ripper.

Martha Turner was out working on Gunthorpe Street with a friend called "Pearly Poll". The women picked up two men in a nearby pub called the White Swan (long since demolished). The two women, with their new clients, stood outside the entrance of Gunthorpe Street (then called George's Yard) and argued over the price for what Pearly Poll later described in her police statement as "a cheap and quick knee trembler". They eventually agreed a price and Martha Turner took her client into the entrance of the Street, under the arch for a bit of privacy. Pearly Poll used the nearby Angel Alley. After fifteen minutes, Pearly Poll had finished; she left for Aldgate and did not see Martha Turner alive again.

At 4.30 am the following morning, a young man called John Reeves left his room in George's Yard Buildings and stumbled over the mutilated body of Martha Turner on the first floor corridor. The modernised flats just on the left, as you enter Gunthorpe Street, are supposed to be the buildings in question. Martha had been stabbed 39 times and her internal organs had been removed and displaced. No one knows what happened to Martha Turner that night. Was it her first client who killed her or did she have another client later that night?

he White Hart Pub: This Pub, which is on the corner of Gunthorpe Street, vas established in 1721. The Pub is very popular and a good place to stop for ome refreshment. This Pub would also have been familiar to the Ripper and his ictims.

irections: Walk a few metres further down Whitechapel High Street, on the eft is Angel Alley 13.

ngel Alley: This Alley has been used extensively by prostitutes (including earl Poll on the night of Martha Turner's murder) and their clients for enturies. There was nowhere else a girl could go for privacy, as most of the vomen were forced into prostitution because they were homeless.

irections: Return to and enter Gunthorpe Street 12. *Walk down Gunthorpe treet to the end where it meets Wentworth Street. Turn left and walk to the ery end where it meets Commercial Street. Turn right along Commercial Street nd on your first right you will see Thrawl Street* 14. *Today only the entrance o the street survives as a new development has been built.*

hrawl Street: This Street has many links with the Ripper and several of his ictims. Mary Ann Nichols, one of his earlier victims lodged (whenever she had he money) at no.18. On the night of her murder, she arrived back at the house runk, only to be turned away for not having the money for a bed for the night. he set out to earn the money on the streets and was later seen heading owards Bucks Row, today called Durward Street 26 where shortly afterwards er mutilated body was found.

Also, here on the corner of this Street, another of the Ripper's victims, Mary ane Kelly, was seen by a friend called George Hutchinson, standing on the orner talking to a man.

As George Hutchinson passed he could see the man put his hand on Mary's houlder. Mary laughed and kissed the stranger. He heard the man say: "You will e alright for what I told you", and Mary replied: "all right". Mary and her new nan walked down Commercial Street to Miller's Court, today named White's ow 16 where the remains of her body were found the next day. The witness aid the man he saw had a heavy moustache and was dressed in a long dark oat, a red neckerchief and was carrying a large black bag!

We will follow the route taken by Mary Nichols and Jack the Ripper as we ead towards the murder site.

irections: Continue along Commercial Street to the corner of Fashion Street 15, *which is the second street on the right.*

ashion Street: This Street, like most of the other streets in this area, was full f slum housing and overcrowded rooms. At least two of the Ripper's victims ived in this Street. The Street would not have changed a great deal since the time of the Ripper except that, where the businesses are today, there would have been seedy lodging houses.

Directions: *Cross over Commercial Street at the zebra crossing. The road directly opposite is called White's Row* **16**.

White's Row: *Murder Site of Mary Jane Kelly*

At the site where today stands a modern car park, in 1888 there stood a narrow alley called Miller's Court, which was a maze of squalid flats and alleys. In one of these flats, the body of Mary Jane Kelly was found. She was heard leaving the flats in the evening singing a song entitled: " Only a Violet Plucked From My Mother's Grave" and she was later seen by a friend on the corner of Thrawl Street, talking to a client whom she brought back to her room, here, at White's Row.

The next morning, a young boy trying to get some rent from Mary, looked into her room through a cracked pane of glass and saw her dissected body. The police were called and they gained access to the house by breaking down the door.

No one was prepared for what they were about to see. At first no one recognised the body as being human. It seemed that Jack the Ripper had spent the entire night with his victim. Using light from a large log fire he had kept burning, he had taken as much time as he needed to finish his job. Mary had been slowly and professionally disembowelled. Her empty carcass lay over her bed; he had removed all her internal organs and intestines and had hung them around the room as if they were Christmas decorations. He then displayed her internal organs on several bedside tables and left her with both her hands tucked up inside her stomach. The whole floor was awash with congealed blood and the officers slipped over onto the floor.

Directions: *Continue along White's Row until the end. Opposite you, on the right, is the Providence Row Night Refuge and Convent* **17**.

Providence Row Night Refuge and Convent: Annie Chapman stayed at the Refuge the night before she was brutally murdered by the Ripper. At the time of her murder she was probably trying to raise enough money to pay for a bed for the following night. This 17th century Refuge is likely to be demolished in 2002.

Directions: *Cross Crispin Street and continue ahead into Artillery Lane* **18**.

Artillery Lane: The house at no. 56 dates from 1756 and is a fine example of the style of housing at that time.

Directions: *Keep to the left and continue ahead into the narrow lane, called Artillery Passage* **19**.

Artillery Passage: Walking down this Passage is like being transported back into Medieval London. Although the shops have been modernised inside, their original exteriors have been retained. During the time of the Ripper, a great deal of London's housing and streets would have looked similar to this.

Directions: Go back down Artillery Passage. Turn left into Artillery Lane and turn first right into Gun Street. Walk to the end. Cross over Brushfield Street and continue on the right. On your left is Spitalfields Market 20. Straight ahead of you is the Parish Church of Spitalfields 21.

Spitalfields Market: Once the home of the London fruit exchange and wool exchange, which was opened in 1929. Today, the building is used as an indoor market with sports and catering facilities. There are refreshments and toilets inside Spitalfields Market.

Directions: Exit Spitalfields Market. Cross over Commercial Street at the traffic lights and on the right is the Parish Church of Spitalfields 21.

Christ Church of Spitalfields: This Church was built in 1714 and would have been a common sight for both the Ripper and his victims, many of whom would walk along this stretch of road looking for clients. The Church was built by Nicholas Hawksmoor and was originally used by the French Huguenots who lived in this area. In the graveyard many of the gravestones have French names.

Directions: On the corner of Fournier Street, adjacent to the Church, is the Ten Bells Pub 22.

Ten Bells Pub: This famous Pub, which was established in 1755, has had many connections with Jack the Ripper. The Pub would have been known and used by all the Ripper's victims, not only as a place to drink, but also as a place of work. Many of the victims worked as prostitutes from inside this pub and would also stand outside looking for any passing trade. Annie Chapman, who was killed in Hanbury Street 23, was working as a prostitute in the Ten Bells Pub on the night she was murdered. It is almost certain that the man she met in the Pub and later left with, was Jack the Ripper himself. Today, the Ten Bells is a safe and friendly Pub. Why not stop here for a swift drink before continuing?

Directions: Turn into Fournier Street.

Fournier Street: This Street has changed very little from the days of the Ripper, except that the houses are in much better condition today. Many of the prostitutes in the 1880s would walk up and down this road trying to get some trade. Notice the houses on the left have window shutters; this is because, during the 18th century, French Huguenot immigrants lived in this area.

Directions: Walk down Fournier Street and turn first left into Wilkes Street. Continue to the end and stop on the right hand side corner where it meets Hanbury Street.

On the opposite side of the road, where the courtyard of the brewery is today, stood no. 29 Hanbury Street **23**.

29 Hanbury Street: ***Murder Site of Annie Chapman.***

Annie Chapman was brutally murdered by Jack the Ripper on the 8th September 1888 after, it is believed, meeting him in the Ten Bells Pub and then bringing him back to a room she had hired at 29 Hanbury Street.

Shortly before her murder, Annie was involved in a very violent fist fight in Dorset Street with a character named "Harry the Hawker". She received bruises and a black eye; there is no record of Harry the Hawker's injuries. Annie was seen before her murder drinking in the Ten Bells Pub and then seen leaving with a male client. A short while after this, she was seen again standing opposite her house on the corner, talking to a man. The man was described to the police as "wearing a black coat and a deerstalker hat and having a shabby appearance". Annie was never seen alive again.

Next morning, John Davies, a neighbour, went down to the backyard through the passage. There he saw the body of Annie, lying close to the backyard steps. He thought she was either drunk or had been raped. Mr Davies is on police record as having said to the police: "I saw a female lying down, her clothing up to her knees and her face covered in blood." He went on to say: "What was lying beside her I cannot describe – it was parts of her body".

Directions: *Turn right along Hanbury Street. Turn right into Brick Lane* **24**.

Brick Lane: Named after a brickworks near here in the 16th century. This area has always been home to immigrants from all over the world: firstly, French Huguenots in the late 1600s; followed by Jewish immigrants from Eastern Europe in the middle 1800s; then, more recently, Bangladeshi people after the Second World War. Today, the street is rich in exotic food, spicy smells, colourful material and all types of shops, even wedding shops. Why not try a good, cheap curry or buy a colourful sari? The Indian sweets are recommended if you like sweet, rich, cakes. Do not be afraid to go inside the shops and look around.

Directions: *Walk down Brick Lane. Every Sunday morning, between dawn and midday, Brick Lane is transformed into one of London's most exciting and famous street markets. It is one of the last few traditional East End markets – full of charm and characters. You will be able to buy almost anything here – clothes, leather goods, bicycles, furniture and second-hand bric-a-brac as well as fruit and vegetables. A good place to pick up a bargain or just enjoy the atmosphere. Continue to the end of Brick Lane where it leads into Osborn Street. Continue to the very end. Turn left into Whitechapel High Street, keeping to the left hand side.*

Continue down Whitechapel High Street. Pass the East London Mosque on the right hand side of the road. Continue further, cross over Vallance Road, which is on your left, then turn into the second road on the left, which is Court Street. Then walk under the bridge. Turn right on the other side of the bridge and in front of you is the Old School **25***, which has now been converted into flats.*

Facing the School, walk to the far left corner of the School and stop at the entrance to Durward Street. Notice how on the right side of Durward Street, the red brickwork of the Old School finishes and the new wall begins. This was once a large wooden gate. Mary Anne Nichols was murdered here at the entrance to this gate **26***.*

Durward Street: ***Murder Site of Mary Anne Nichols***

Mary was officially the first victim of the Ripper. Mary was described as a drab 44-year old street prostitute; her street name was "Polly". On 31st August 1888, the night of her murder, she was living in Thrawl Street **14** *with three other prostitutes. After drinking heavily, she returned to her lodgings where she was refused entry because she did not have her "doss money" for that night ("doss" is slang for sleep).*

One hour later, she was seen by a friend drunkenly walking along Whitechapel High Street. She boasted to her friend that she had made three times her doss money today, but had drank it. Her friend remembered that the bells of Christ Church of Spitalfields rang out at 2.30 am.

At 3.30 am, Charlie Cross was making his way to work as a market porter. He entered Durward Street and noticed what looked like a bundle of clothes in the gateway. He had a closer look and saw the body of Polly. She was lying partly on the road and partly on the pavement; her skirt had been pulled up. Minutes later, a policeman arrived, and, using his torch, they discovered a horrific scene. Polly's throat had been cut from ear-to-ear in an attempt, it appeared, to cut off her head. She was still warm and blood was oozing from her wounds.

A doctor was called; he agreed that she was dead – not the most difficult diagnosis, as the poor woman had also been gutted and filleted like a fish. Polly was later identified by her ex-husband, who bent over her mutilated body and said:"I forgive you, as you are, for what you have done to me".

Directions: *As you return to Whitechapel High Street the way you came, look out for the narrow road on the far side of the School, called Winthorpe Street. During the 17th century, this Street used to be called Ducking Pond Row. Here, wives who had scorned their husbands were taken to a pond at the end of the Street and tied to wooden chairs; the women would be ducked into the water as a punishment, and they sometimes drowned.*

Return to Whitechapel High Street. Turn left. On the opposite side of the Street is the London Hospital **27**.

London Hospital: Built and opened in 1757 and heavily bomb-damaged in the Blitz, this Hospital still serves the local area and its poor, as was its main aim when the Hospital was first established. It was in this Hospital that Joseph Merrick (who was known as **"the Elephant Man"** lived in safety, and where today his remains are still kept in the Hospital Museum (not open to the public).

Directions: *Continue a little further on the left and stop outside no. 259 Whitechapel High Street* **28***, which is directly opposite the main entrance and steps of the London Hospital.*

No. 259 Whitechapel High Street: Today, this building is a sari shop. However, during 1889, this building housed a gruesome waxworks at the front of the shop, containing (amongst other things) the waxwork models of the Ripper's victim's bodies. Also, at the back of the shop, behind the waxworks, was a freak show. The main attraction at this freak show, in a cage at the very back of the building, was Joseph Merrick, aged only 25 years and who was called **the Elephant Man** by the freak show owner, because of the appalling disfigurements to Merrick's entire face and most of his body.

Merrick was kept in a dark cage and, whenever people paid to come into the show, he was ordered like a dog to stand and take off his hood and clothes, made to show his mutilated face and stand naked in front of the crowd. At certain times of the day, Merrick also stood in the window at the front of the building, his face and body covered, so as to entice passing members of the public into the show. There was even a picture of Merrick hanging outside on the wall.

Luckily for Joseph Merrick, this freak show was directly opposite the main entrance of the London Hospital and one day Dr Treves, a famous pathologist, saw Merrick at this window. Dr Treves had an interest in skin disorders and went into the freak show. Eventually, he "bought" Merrick from the owner of the show and moved Merrick into the London Hospital. Treves believed and hoped that Merrick was an imbecile, because of the sad and lonely life he had lived. However, it soon became obvious that Merrick was highly intelligent and had taught himself to read using only the Bible. Merrick became famous in High Society London; even the then-current Princess of Wales visited Merrick in his private bedroom in the nurses' quarters in the Hospital.

Merrick died in 1890, lying on his back in bed. Lying down in such a manner was something that he knew was dangerous and would probably kill him, due to the fact that his head was so enlarged and deformed. However, all his life Merrick had craved to be able to sleep "like other people".